Milonia (Milon) V. Parker embarked on her career in modeling in 2005 at the age of 26, when she was approached by Jennifer Griffin of Journey Creative to model in the Hard Candy Stud Calendar for charity. Milon's enthusiasm, professionalism and passion, propelled the calendar to a huge success. Milon has modeled for numerous of different types of print work.

Milon's edgy, androgynous look and open lesbian lifestyle has made her the perfect pictorial representation of pride through out the L.G.B.T community in the Midwest.

In July 2008 Milon was the focus of a three part diversified marketing campaign for Ultr E!go Magazine, which included a full-length themed photo shoot and interview. In December 2008, Milon was in her first fashion show at Macy's Downtown Chicago on State St for A.I.D.S Awareness. As a follow up to her December showcasing Milon has walked the runway in Blake Martin's Vanity Nights fashion show and many more showcases where she was chosen by different designers that wanted to break the mold of what a "Female" model should and could wear on the runway and they all ended up being a sold out affair. Milon continues to make her mark on Chicago's up and coming fashion scene.

Milon has been a passionate writer/poet every since high school. Milon is very dedicated to not only delivering enticing material, but also conveying a message of validity and purpose.

Who Was She ?

A Poetry book

By

Milonia V. Parker

Editor

lolajames

Copyright © 2009 by Milonia Venus Parker

Published by lulu.com

All rights reserved.

Reproduction or translation of any part of this work beyond that permitted by Section 107 or 108 of the 1976 United States Copyright Act without the permission of the copyright owner is unlawful. Requests for permission or further information should be addressed to miloniaparker@yahoo.com

This publication is designed to provide the reader with a fictional story that will require them to think about their actions. It is no way, shape or form a recapture of true events or people. It is truly a fictional piece of work.

Library of Congress Cataloging-in-Publication Data:

Milonia Venus Parker

Who Was She? / Milon Parker

p. cm.-

ISBN 978-0-557-05286-8

Printed in the United States of America

For more information on Milon's artistic work please feel free to visit her website at:

www.themakingsofmvp.com

www.myspace.com/infamousmvp1

www.youtube.com/milon1

www.modelmayhem.com/milon

or you can email her at:

miloniaparker@yahoo.com

My Thank You's

This accomplishment is in honor of God, for without him nothing is possible, Carolyn Gumm, my mother for her support and encouragement, Lea Royster, CEO of Ultr E!go, for giving me ideas and letting me put the beginnings of "Who Was She?" onto her website for exposure, Demetrius "Fresh The Model" Harris, asst. front cover illustrator, for his countless hours of dedication and combining his graphic design talent with mine to create a compelling front cover, Quintella Johnson, my dear friend, for helping me along the way and giving me the advice and steps on getting it done, *lolajames*, my editor, for her undying effort to see my vision become reality, Jennifer Griffin, my photographer, for her optimism and patience, my good friend officer Jim Goulakos and everyone else who has been with me from the inception to the completion. Here it is. The moment you all have been waiting on- in its entirety. I hope you enjoy!

To everyone who has been continuously interested in knowing more about "Who Was She?" this couldn't have been done without your help, support, belief and trust.

It is you I thank!

THIS IS NOT A TRUE STORY!! The characters names in the book have not been changed to protect the innocent and none of the events described in this book are real. This is strictly a fictional piece with the intention of enticing the reader to think about their actions and its effects on others. It has been a creative outlet for me and a means of satisfaction for my altruistic itch.

TABLE OF CONTENTS

I. Pleasure First   1

II. High Time Surprise   5

III. Lesson Thought   9

IV. Realization   17

V. Full Frontal   23

VI. Reveal/ation   27

VII. Relentless Pursue   31

VIII. Again   35

IX. The Fate Of The Wait   41

X. Drama   45

XI. Femme Reality   49

XII. Time Waits For No One   51

XIII. Compassionary Measures   55

Testimonies   61

Scrapbook/poem   67

I

PLEASURE FIRST

There are times when all you can see is the pleasure you will feel when your senses are satisfied...the journey begins...

I pulled up to the club valet parked of course
feeling good about myself. No negative feelings,
and no remorse   I could
hear the music as I approached the club Jeezy
spitting on Usher's new joint "Have you
ever made love to a thug"?
I walked in the club through the crowd toward
the bar
All eyes on me, as if I was a movie star
I ordered me a long island ice tea, took a sip it
went down real smooth
I looked around the club and noticed how
crowded it was
Like damn I couldn't even move
I glanced across the room at a female that I had
never seen before

She had this intriguing sex appeal about herself when she walked through the door

About 5'1" light skinned, long hair, medium body not too thick, not too thin...

As she walked in my direction, that's when I started to grin

Because once I get her to grin

I'm in

G-A-M-E begin

She was so sexy, body looking like an amusement park that I would love to play in I'm usually an outside person, but with her she definitely would have me stay in

I approached her

"Hey how you doing sweetheart?"

Little did I know that the game was about to start

She grinned and replied

> "I'm doing just fine."

I asked if I could buy her a drink, preferably a bottle of wine

She laughed and said

> "You don't have to buy me wine to impress me."

All you have to do is figure out who I am, and what I want in order to undress me
I thought to myself, like damn I like that
As a matter of fact, why don't you explain to me how I can do that?
She moved in front of me so no one would see
Exactly what it was that she was about to do to me

She pulled me to her and began kissing my lips

She took my left hand and put it in her panties

And placed my right hand on her hips

As I began rubbing her clitoris, her juices began to flow

Fingering her in, out, back, and forth real slow

Just as she climaxed, she took my hand out and sucked my fingers until the juices were gone

At that point I was very aroused, throbbing and turned on
She whispered in my ear, I'm going to the restroom I won't be long
Five minutes turned into three hours I never saw her again

*But **WAIT** that was just the beginning*

II
HIGH TIMES SURPRISE

In an escape from curiosity we venture into the world of the unknown seeking what peaks our interest...the unknown pursuit...

I hopped in my truck
The sun was shining so bright on my windshield
Daydreaming, I let three cars drive past as I sat there to yield

I made a left turn and jumped on the expressway
The news said that it would be clear skies pretty much all day
So I headed to the mall to buy me a new pair of shorts so I can ball
I can hoop my ass off even though I'm not that tall

Pulled up to the store, took my keys out of the ignition then closed my truck door

As I walked through the store I couldn't believe my eyes,

So I took a second glance, which caught me by surprise

It was the chic from the club that I hadn't seen in a week

I'm not letting her get away this time without trying to speak
I wanted to call out to her but she never told me her name
She noticed me watching her full of confidence rather than shame

She smiled at me as she went inside the dressing room

I thought to myself

"She wants me to follow her in I assume"

So I grabbed a t-shirt and a pair of shorts
Told the worker I wanted to try these on
She told me room #4 and if I needed any help her name was Shawn

Oblivious to what she said
I rushed towards the dressing rooms to look for the mysterious chic that already had me gone in the head

I tried peaking in each room trying to find that mysterious chic

Anticipating that she would open her door rather than have me pick
Room #3 opened, she grabbed my arm and pushed me toward the wall
After she began unbuttoning my pants, she then made my boxers fall
She placed her two fingers on the tip of my clit
Moving my lips apart as she began to lick

I grabbed the back of her head, as she slid her tongue back and forth in between my legs

She was so into it I could tell she had an appetite and wanted to be fed
It felt so good, but I wanted her to stop
I couldn't help how she was making me feel uncontrollably hot

I was about to cum, so I tried to stop her the best way I could
The thought of me not knowing her made it feel better than just good

"Oh shit! I'm Cumming!!!"

My juices flowed all down her lips
I must have tasted good to her, because she started licking her fingertips
I stood there with my eyes closed, in disbelief and exhaustion
Because crazy shit like that didn't happen to me often

Embarrassed and intrigued all at the same time

Thoughts of

"How did I get myself into this?"

Was racing rapidly through out my mind
As I opened my eyes to finally find out who was this chic that had led me on
That's when no one appeared before me
Once again she was

GONE...

However she left a note behind that said her name was Dee
Guess I'll find out who she is, in Part III

III
LESSON THOUGHT

It is when we think we know what we are doing when we realize we were swayed by mystery...it happened...

It was a quarter to midnight
Not an image in sight
Besides the moon all I saw was passing cars and their front headlights
I laid across my bed with my hands behind my head
Contemplating if I should go out or stay in the crib instead
I thought

"The odds of me running into this chic again are slim if I stay inside"

I guess I'll throw something on, put my "STRAP ON", and go for a ride

I drove around the town with my windows rolled down
No tint on my front windows so I could be seen now

I stopped at a red light as a vehicle approached me from the rear
You could hear them switching the acceleration system to third gear

The light turned green so I stepped on the gas
The vehicle that was behind me, switched lanes and drove pass
I have a V8 so I'm thinking,

"Ok what was that for?"

I know they don't want to race
The car then slowed down next to me, so I could see their face

It was that mysterious chic Dee who I didn't know and who definitely didn't know me

Where did she come from and how did she know where I would be?

At that point it didn't even matter anymore
As she sped off I chased her down 71st and Lake Shore
She dipped through the park, jumped out her car, ran and went to hide in the dark
I pulled up behind her car so that she couldn't get away this time

I just wanted to know who she was even if she didn't want to be mine

I walked through the park toward the water by the bay
She came out of nowhere grabbed me from behind and said

"Hey!"

I turned around and smiled at her as she began to kiss me
I stopped her and asked, *"If you're so into me then why do you continue to diss me?"*

She put her index finger over my lip and told me to be silent

She put her hand in my boxers and told me to FUCK the shit out of her as if we were on a deserted island

She grinded on my strap with a face so serious
So I began unbuttoning my pants cause I to was curious.
I laid her on the grass before releasing my hands from her ass

Then slid the head of my strap in her as she pulled her panties to the side

After I fucked the shit out of her she got on top of me so she could ride

She rode me so long she came about three times and then four

Just as I thought she was done she said

"Don't stop 1 more!!!"

After she came she grabbed my strap and began licking all over the dick
She was lying sideways so that gave me access to finger her and play with her clit
She began sucking my strap like she was a pro
Slapping herself with it then sticking it all the way in her throat *fast and then slow*
I was ready to cum just by seeing her in action

This bitch was more than a freak sucking dick was her passion

She took my strap off so that we could grind
Then she placed her pussy on top of mine

I could feel her warm wet pussy throbbing as we grinded as one
I was so worked up from fucking her already I was about to cum
I closed my eyes tightly as my juices exploded all over hers and on me
As I opened them all I could see were her and the silhouette of a tree

I laid there with so many questions floating through my mind
Wanting to ask her, but I didn't want her to hush me again like last time
So I just laid there with her head on my chest
As my fingertips roamed the side of her breast
I could tell that this girl had a story and had a lot to express
But I really wanted to know if she does this with everyone and if not what makes me different from the rest

She finally lifted her head and began to stare at me
I asked her if she had anything in particular that she would like to share with me

She just looked at me with no expression not even a blink
The more I looked at her she looked familiar so then I began to think

With anger in her voice she asked

    You don't remember me what so ever do you?

I said

    "No, not at all but could you at least give me a clue?"

She said we met online about three years ago or a little more
I came to meet you for the first time, but you never opened your door

Back then I had lied that picture wasn't me that I posted on the internet

I was over weight and if I had been honest with you then we would have never met

As tears began to run down her face I began to worry what else was about to take place my mind full of confusion I asked Dee

"Why are you crying?"

She angrily replied and said

"Because of me you too are dying!"

In a frantic voice, I said what the fuck do you mean I'm dying?

I know I hurt you in the past, but if your goal was to scare me, I'm scared so you can stop trying

She stood up over me with her 22 semi-automatic gun
She said now I can tell you the truth because my work here is now done
She said Karma is a bitch I have H.I.V and I'm not lying
Now I'm in this fucked up situation all because I was intrigued by a pretty face and a chase now I too, pretty soon will be dying
I just sat there, worried and confused thinking how could this be?
The bitch that I had been chasing was a stalker who had just infected me with H.I.V everything that glitters is not gold **REALTALK**!!

But wait you thought this was the end, it's still the beginning stay tuned

IV
REALIZATION
Being caught in an unfortunate situation makes us regret our choices...it hit me

As she walked away, she had just told me the worst news of my life
I couldn't help but regret having sex with her, knowing that it wasn't right
All I could think about was,

"If she didn't have that gun I would have fucked her up"

This wasn't just a bad night and it was far from bad luck
Finally I got up from the grass
As I approached my car that's when she drove pass

She laughed at me and told me,

"Oh now! Don't look so pathetic"

Even though I tried not to let it affect me I couldn't help but let it

Once I got in my truck and turned the radio on I couldn't believe my ears when I heard that particular song

"I said it's too late to apologize, it's too late"

Damn I'm so stupid now I'm dying and going to start losing weight

I didn't want to tell any of my friends
So I called my mom

I told her

"I'm about to come over there so leave the porch light on"

When I got there before I could tell her what happened, I started crying

She asked me

"Is everything ok?"

I replied

"No mom! I'm dying!"

She said Dying? What are you talking about?
I was so ashamed to tell her, but if I didn't eventually she would have found out
As I began to explain to her what was going on, her telephone started ringing
It's 3 in the morning, who could that be I started thinking?

My mom picked up the phone and said who is this calling my house this damn late
The caller on the other end started laughing and saying,

"I just used your daughter for bait!"

She hung up the phone in my mothers face
And from the look on my mothers face
I wasn't ready for what was about to take place

She started yelling at me and asking me what the hell is going on
Don't tell me you brought some bullshit into my home

With tears in my eyes, I said mom I've made a terrible mistake
I met this psychotic chic online trying to find a date

I know it sounds desperate, but my friend and her wife met online
I still went on there even though you tried to warn me when I went on there every time
But when they met, I thought it was a sign

Because they ended up being each others soul mate,
And I thought maybe I could find mine
For about two whole minutes my mom just looked at me with anger in her eyes

But it wouldn't be until I told her the sexual part of the story that she would be very surprised...

V
FULL FRONTAL

Confronted with the stress society puts on physical appearance leads us to superficial involvement and an even deeper emotional scar for those targeted...could this be my punishment? The plot thickens...

My mom said

"What does meeting this crazy chic online have to do with you dying?"

I said because well mom here's the whole story of how I met this chic online:

"My friend Carrie was single so she went on Ultre E!go's dating website
Ironically she met a girl named Tonya on there the same night

They talked for awhile and then marriage came about
That's when Tonya then moved into Carrie's house they were so happy and excited that they found each other I was eager to meet someone on there to but I procrastinated because of you mother
You always tried to warn me about meeting people online
Because I don't know what kind of person they are and they could be out of their mind
Of course I didn't want to hear what you were talking about
But eventually if I would have listened I would not have had to find out
So one day I was online and met this chic named Dee
We talked for about 3 weeks so I could get to know her and she could get to know me
The pictures that she had on her profile showed a chic with a nice body and she was so fine
I was so excited to meet her I called off work so we could meet the next morning around nine

That morning my stomach was hurting as I got dressed
I continued to put my hottest outfit on so that she would be impressed
As I finished getting dressed there was a knock on the door
I went to the door excited but when I looked through the peep hole I wasn't anymore
What I saw was a short fat chic standing there
The only thing that looked good on her was her light complexion and her pretty hair
I jumped as she knocked on the door again I could tell that she was getting very impatient cause I wouldn't let her in
She knocked once more and said

"I know you're home you just don't want to let me in because I'm fat"

I thought to myself

"Yea you're definitely right about that!"

She stood in front of my crib hurt for about 10 minutes"

Little did my mom know that this was part of the story

But was only the beginning...

VI
REVEAL/ATION
When we reveal and revel in our mistakes that's when we learn the greatest lessons...schooled

As I started getting into details of how we met again and had sex this time
That's when my mom stopped me and said ok that's enough I can read in between the lines
My mother became speechless because of what I told her that happened
But about two minutes later it must have sunk in because that's when she started snapping

She asked me how could I be so irresponsible and so damn naivc

I don't think you caught it, until the doctor diagnosis you with it that's when I'll believe
So we started looking through phone books to find a clinic

We made an appointment
But the day of my visit I was too embarrassed to go in it
Ashamed, I walked in and told the receptionist what my appointment was for
I signed in then ten minutes later the nurse told me to go in the room that had a 2 on the door
As I sat in the room I saw posters of people with AIDS on the wall
It showed them sick, dying and how they use to be bigger and how they'd turned small

I tried to joke about it saying if fat people want to lose weight all they have to do is catch that shit

Then reality hit me. That's not funny having AIDS isn't anything to play with
Then crazy thoughts flowed through my mind like what if I really do have H.I.V?
All because I met a chic online that wasn't my type and now she wanted revenge on me

The doctor knocked on the door and asked if he could come in
He asked me what seems to be the problem.
I said where do you want me to begin?

After I told him the story he took my blood and when he was done I was too hurt to speak
He said your results would be back in a little over a week

I said a week? Is there any kind of way that I can find out today?
He said No! This is only the second week in April it normally wouldn't be ready until May
With anger in my voice I said Ok! Are you going to call me or will I have to call you?
The doctor told me to calm down when I get the results back I'll call you so you can Come back through
Before I exited out of the doctor's office I asked the doctor if I really did catch it can I
Sue?

He said yea if you know for sure who gave it to you?
He must not have believed my story because I already told him that I knew
At that point I wanted to find her just to hear what all she had to say
But this time I'm going to be strapped with an actual gun, unlike I was the other day

I went to the gun store and purchased me a nine
Because I'm not letting her catch me off guard like last time
So I rode around town searching through every restaurant and bar
It was only a matter of time before I found her at a Mc Donald's parking lot sitting in her car

Heart racing feet pacing just what am I going to do now?

VII
RELENTLESS PURSUE

In our futile attempts to lose ourselves in blaming someone else we are denying the fact that we've caused our own effects...this is a different kind of chase

My heart started racing fast once I saw the same exact car she was in
If it was her I knew I had better hurry up then
So I jumped out of my truck with my gun at my waist
I put a hoody on so she couldn't see my face
As I approached her passenger side window I pointed my gun at her head
Too bad it wasn't her it was someone else instead
The woman frantically screamed and cried out please don't shoot me I'm a mother and a wife
I told her I'm not going to hurt you, your car fit the description of someone I was with last night

So I got back in my truck upset and shaking
I hadn't eaten all day so my stomach was aching
I pulled off trying to decide what I was going to eat
I'm picky when it comes to food because I don't eat red meat

So I went to this placed called Chicken and Things
I ordered me some fries, a drink and five wings
I took it to go because I didn't want to eat there
It was too many begging bums around and I wasn't in the mood to share

On the drive home I kept replaying how I got into this fucked up situation
And how I still can't believe I had sex with her with out any hesitation

I can honestly say that I didn't know that I could catch H.I.V. from having sex with another female
And if she really did give it to me she's going to end up dead or in jail

As I drove home I continued to see if I could find her
But from being up all night my eyes began to blur
By this time it was a quarter to one
I started nodding off and that's when I knew the search was done

So I went home and as soon as I crawled into my bed that's when my phone rang
As I answered it the same caller that called my moms house was laughing so I told her

"This isn't a game!"

She said you know what you're right this isn't a game

"But since I'm not sure who gave it to me someone's got to take the blame"

VIII
AGAIN

When faced with adversity some coward and some walk right up to it with an unshakeable confidence, but what happens when both emotions completely takes over?...faltered

I asked her
"Why do I have to be the one to blame??
I wasn't the one that took away your sunshine and gave you rain
I'm as innocent as you are as well
Did you know by doing this to people you're going to go straight to jail?"

She sat quietly on the phone listening to what I had to say
I thought I was reeling her in so I asked her if we could meet at the forest preserve the next day.

She quickly said
NO! You sent me off way back then!
How do I know you're not trying to send me off again??
I told her I really need for us to sit down and talk everything through
I promise I'll be there and won't try to harm you
I just have some questions that I need to ask
Mainly about your life and your past
But before I could finish

She hung up on me fast!

Five minutes later my phone rang again
She said OK! We can meet Thursday night at the forest preserve around ten
When we got off the phone I went right to sleep
I must have been exhausted because I didn't wake up the next day until around three

That day was Wednesday one more day for us to meet
She just don't know that this time I'm going to be prepared because I'm bringing some heat

I was kind of depressed so I didn't want to go outside
My friends kept asking me what's wrong
The more they asked, the more I lied

I stayed in the house watching reruns of good times
The more I saw H.I.V commercials on TV the more my results stayed on my mind
I finally turned off the TV and went to bed
As I dreamed all kinds of things were going through my head
I even dreamed that I saw myself in a coffin lying there emotionless and dead
I was having a nightmare in actuality
It was about everyone knowing that I had H.I.V and they were laughing at me

I kept waking up in cold sweats through out the night
Trying to find some kind of way to get my mind right
So I got some sleeping pills and went into the kitchen to get something to drink
I didn't have anything in the refrigerator so I had to get some water from the sink

After I took the pills, I went to lay back down
Hoping that I could finally get some sleep now

As I slept like a baby Thursday night finally came
I got up and got dressed because I heard what sounded like rain
When I finally looked at the clock I noticed that I was running late
And if she got there and didn't see me I'm sure she wasn't going to wait

The time now was 8:30 and it would take me and hour and a half to get there

So when I got on the expressway I started
speeding and if the police would have saw me I
would not have cared

When I got there it was five minutes to ten
I sat back in the cut so I could see what kind of
vehicle she would be in

That way I could get her plate number
It was now 10 o'clock and she still wasn't there
so I began to wonder

Was she really going to show up or did she lie to
me
Just as I said that a car pulled in the park with their
bright on, so that I couldn't see

The lights blinded me so bad I felt like I wasn't
going to be able to see anymore
She pulled up right next to me turned her engine
off and opened her drivers door

IX
THE FATE OF THE WAIT

It is when we act hastily in a situation we caused that we find ourselves in a deeper mess than when we first started...in above my head

As she opened her door she ordered for me to get out of my car first
When I got out and closed my door she told me to lift up my shirt
So I lifted my shirt up far enough for her to see
Then she told me to pull my pants legs up to my knees
Luckily before I got there I took my gun off and placed it on the floor
When she noticed that I didn't have anything she got out of her car and closed the door

She said

"OK! Now what all would you like to know?"

I said

"I wouldn't like anything at this point but to know why are you running around town like a hoe?"

She said excuse me?

*"No! I am not a hoe, nor do I go around having sex with everyone
I was intrigued just like you were, looking for fun
But instead my fun back fired in my face
All because it was different to me, and I also love a chase
But I mainly focused on you because I knew that you were naive
And was too caught up in the moment to see what plans I had up my sleeve*

On top of that if I gave it to you then you could help me spread it to everyone
Then once you gave it to the majority of the gay community then my job was done
That's why I told your mother I used you as bait
Plus you should have never stood me up the day of our date"

In an angrily loud tone I told her

"You should have not lied about how you look and I don't deserve this!"

She told me to

"Stop getting so loud you're making me nervous!!"

I said nervous well I'm way beyond that
I'm tired of talking enough of this chitchat
I pulled out some mace from my boot sprayed her in the face then ran to my car to get my gat

With mace in her eyes she still managed to fire her gun at me
As she fired in my direction I hit the ground and hid behind a tree
When she kept firing at me she must have ran out of bullets
Because every time she tried to fire at me no bullets came out as she pulled it
I crawled on my hands and knees until I got to my truck
When I tried to open the door I couldn't the handle was stuck
Just as I got the door open she started shooting at me again but she missed each time
Finally I picked my gun up from off the floor and began firing mine
As she kept firing at me I kept firing back
Not sure if I shot her but she began running into the woods which was pitch black
Right when I was about to run in the woods after her four police cars pulled up

All I could say now was what the fuck!!!

X
DRAMA

Flashing lights are presumed by many as a confirmation that they have arrived but the ride there is always not as good as anyone could have ever dreamed...scene 10 act 11...life over

THE POLICE JUMPED OUT OF THEIR CARS WITH THEIR GUNS OUT AND TOLD ME TO FREEZE

Then they told me to put my hands behind my back and drop to my knees
So I complied with what they told me to do
Then my mom got out of the police car telling me I had them to follow you
She also told me that she told the police about everything that had happened
I should have known my mom had some juice because her ex husband was a police captain

After the police went into the woods to find her
me and my mom left and went to my mom's
home
I was too shaken up and wasn't in the mood to
be all alone
As I sat in the front room at her place
The news came on saying that a woman had
been shot to death but they wouldn't disclose her
information or her face
Immediately I got excited and then I got scared
I thought I should go view the body but I knew I
wasn't mentally prepared

So I just sat there wondering if it was her or not
that had been shot
Or was this just another one of her games or
plots
Either way I looked at the situation if I killed her
it was good and bad
And if the results came back positive that's going
to be the worst news in my life I've ever had

So as days went past I kept thinking about what
my results would be
Hoping and praying that she didn't really infect me
with H.I.V
There was one more day left until I got the big
news
But if I do or don't have it no matter what if she's
dead, I still lose
I loose because I took the law into my own hands
And me taking someone's life wasn't part of
God's plan
I fell asleep praying then woke up the next
morning around eight
My mom could tell I was worried about my
results so she told me not to worry just have
faith
The doctor finally called me around 9:30
He told me to hurry up and get there because
today he was leaving early
So we got dressed jumped in my ride and we got
there in ten minutes
*My doctor was standing in the lobby with the nurse
as I walked into the clinic*

XI
FEMME REALITY

stricken with fear, depression and haste is usually times when our entire lives flash before our face...it could all end with one mistake...this really can't be...

My heart immediately began beating fast when I saw them standing there
Praying that they didn't have any bad news to share
My doctor said

"Good morning! How do you feel today?"

I told him that

"I was ready to get the results out of the way."

Then he said
"I'll be with you in a moment go have a seat."

The more we sat there as he talked to the nurse my heart began to feel weak
I wasn't sure what they were talking about I just hoped that it wasn't about me
And if it was hopefully they were saying how I didn't have H.I.V

It seemed like we had been sitting there for so long

I really wished that he would hurry up and bring his ass on

Finally he finished talking to the nurse and told me to follow him into his room
By him taking so long to get to me he had good news I assumed
So I followed him in and he closed the door then sat in his chair
He then said are you ready for the important news that I'm about to share??
As tears ran down my face I said yes
So he then began opening up the envelope to reveal the results of my test

XII
TIME WAITS FOR NO ONE
Not mothers, daughters, friends or foe it is reality that we have to think carefully before we enter into a situation that will not only effect ourselves but everyone around us...what have I done?

As HE began LIFTING the FLAP to OPEN the ENVELOPE that THE test RESULTS were IN

I COULDN'T help BUT think ABOUT my MOTHER my FAMILY and FRIENDS

I WONDERED if I had IT would THEY still BE by MY side

OR be UPSET because THEY kept ASKING me WHAT was WRONG and I lied

WHEN he PULLED the PIECE of PAPER out HE told ME no MATTER which WAY this MAY go

IF you DO have IT I JUST want YOU to KNOW that I can GIVE you SOME medication BEFORE you GO

I ANGRILY said

"DOC could YOU please JUST read THE fucking PAPER!?!"

If YOU don't MIND I WOULD like TO know NOW not LATER

He SAID ok! OK! i'm NERVOUS just LIKE you

JUST as HE was ABOUT to READ it THERE was A knock ON the DOOR before HE could EVEN start TO

it WAS my MOTHER who HAD knocked ON the DOOR

with TEARS in HER eyes SHE asked IF there WAS room FOR one MORE

i SMILED as SHE came INTO the ROOM she
GAVE me A big HUG and TOLD me THAT i
WASN'T alone

WHEN she SAID that I could TELL she WAS
nervous ALSO from HER tone

WHEN he FINALLY was ABOUT to READ the
RESULTS i TOLD him I don't THINK i REALLY
wanna KNOW

so I tried TO leave BUT my MOM stopped ME
and SAID please LET him TELL you BEFORE
you GO
she SAID that WAY if YOU do HAVE it YOU
won't INFECT anyone AND can GET some
MEDICATION

instead THE doctor GAVE the RESULTS to MY
mother AND she TOOK it WITH out ANY
hesitation

XIII
COMPASSIONARY MEASURES

It's acquired through time and is the result of the desire to treat another being with respect; compassion is a focus on someone other than yourself...which road will you choose?

After the doctor handed my results to my mother to read he left the room
Because my mom was about to read it it was good news I assumed

My mother told me the results and said "indeed I was infected"

And that I hate to say this but I hope now you've learned your lesson
I didn't believe the results so I had her read them to me again
As she read it I started crying because a new life was about to begin

All those times my mom tried to warn me I thought
she didn't understand and was just tripping
Now look at me infected with H.I.V all because I
didn't listen
Now I have a new life that I'm about to lead
And I could forget about having kids because I
would pass it to my seed
I and my mother left the clinic and I dropped her
off at home
I told her I'll be back in a little while I need time
to think and want to be left alone
She said ok I understand but when you get back we
really need to talk
I said ok I'm going to the park up the street to
take a walk
So I dropped her off and went on my way

***It would be hours later until I did the
unthinkable on that day***

I went to the park, sat there for hours crying and then loaded my gun
I said to myself I can't believe I lost so that means that Dee won
Whether she was still alive or dead
In a suicide state of mind I raised my right hand with the gun in it and pointed it at my head
I placed the tip of the gun right on my right temple
I thought that I could pull the trigger but it wasn't that simple
As I sat there my mother called me but I didn't answer the phone
I already told her that I just wanted to be left alone

I lowered the gun and laid it on my lap and starting crying again and saying that my life is over this is the end
Then I angrily wiped my tears and pointed my gun back at my head again

Bang!!!!!

That's right
I really did shoot myself in the head that night
I did it because I wasn't about to go on living with H.I.V and in jail
Because whether I killed myself or not I would still be living in hell
As you can see I must not be dead
Because, if I was none of this part of the story you could have read
Unfortunately, when I shot myself in the head the bullet didn't kill me
It just took away part of my speech, brain and walking ability
However when I left the clinic my mom tried to tell me the truth when she called me to disclose what my actual results were
But she had no idea what was about to occur

See my mother and the doctor had played a trick on me. The doctor put false results in the envelope because my mother asked him to. She wanted me to learn my lesson because I didn't listen to her like she always told me to, but it back fired on them they thought I was only going to be upset and accept that I had it and go on living. However, instead I tried to take my life. As far as Dee, she really did get her revenge on me, because now that I'm disabled, no one will ever want me.

To all internet users out there teenagers or adults
Be careful who you meet online and peoples feelings that you hurt!
BECAUSE THEY MAY SEEM LIKE THEY HAVE YOUR BEST INTEREST AT HEART BUT IN REALITY THAT MAY NOT BE THE CASE.

TESTIMONIES

Here are real stories/testimonies similar to the book you just read.

Testimony #1

"I am a 26 year old homosexual male and I contracted H.I.V. at the age of 20. I've been living with it for 6 years. I caught H.I.V. from an ex boyfriend. My ex told me he gave it to me on purpose. His reason was because he loved me and didn't want me to ever leave him. When I brought it to him a heated argument turned into a vicious fight. I tried to leave before hand because I was done with him so the argument became very violent."

Questions:

Since you've caught H.I.V. how has it changed your life?

"Even though getting involved into the life style I knew about the pros and cons I still pursued it. I was comfortable with it because I grew up with relatives that were H.I.V. positive . But I was still careless because I was young. And when I found out that I caught it I was still hurt and felt like I wouldn't be with anyone else again."

Do you think marriage between consenting homosexuals would possibly help prevent H.I.V.?

"No, I disagree because a lot of marriages don't last long. In marriages they cheat even if their straight or gay. Being married won't prevent H.I.V. It's about being cautious and safe with anyone you come in contact with married or not."

If you could say anything to the listeners out there whether they're gay/straight, young or older concerning what you've been through, what would it be?

"I would say trust no one unless u actually know that person completely, their ins and outs."

"Also, never be temped or caught up in temptation because it might seriously hurt you in the long run, TEMPTATION is a win or loose situation."

Testimony #2

"I'm a 17 year old homosexual female that learned my lesson from meeting people over the phone and on MySpace. In 2007 I met a female on a party line. A party line is where you meet people in chat rooms over the phone. We lived in two different states so all we could do was talk on the phone. We talked on the phone for a year and we still hadn't seen each other. Every time I came to town she always made up an excuse not to see me. One day she told me that she had got raped and ended up getting pregnant as the result. By this time I loved her so I stayed with her. Eventually we both ended up getting MySpace pages. She had pictures of how she looked on there. Pictures of when she wasn't pregnant and pictures of her stomach getting bigger from being pregnant. I came to town one day and she was supposed to bring me some shoes to my grandmothers' house. Instead, she had her sister drop them off. She said that she had something to do that's why her sister brought them over for her. At first I didn't think anything of it. But as time went on I kept asking to see her when I would come to town to visit my family. My older cousin use to laugh at me because she thought I made up this girl. So I came back to town. It was 2008 by this time. We had been together for over a year and hadn't seen each other

still. When I came to town I told her that I was about to come see her. But she didn't want to see me. She begged for me not to come over. I lied and told her that I wasn't coming then. So I had my cousin take me over her house anyway. We popped up at her house anyway. My cousin stayed in the car as I went to knock on the door. Mind u we were still on the phone she didn't know I was at her door. So when I knocked on the door her sister that brought me those shoes open the door and let me in. At this point she knew I was there and wouldn't open the bathroom door where she was. So her sister busted the door open. When the door opened, I couldn't believe my eyes so I ran out the house towards my cousin's car. I told her to drive off. She asked me "what was wrong?" She was ready to fight because she thought someone tried to hurt me. She eventually drove off and that's when I told her what happened. The girl I met on the party line had lied about who she was, how she looked and about being pregnant. My cousin started laughing at me. At first I was very angry but then I started laughing also.

To sum it up the pictures that she had on her MySpace page was pictures of her best friend. She and her best friend were both in on it. She lied about how she looked because she was ashamed that she was over weight, knew that she wasn't my type and didn't think I would still be with her."

QUESTIONS:

Where you angry when you found out that she had lied about who she was and how she looked?

"Yes, I was very angry and hurt because I was in love with her and she lied to me".

Have you learned your lesson? And would you go on another party line or meet someone off MySpace with out knowing for sure if it's really them again?

"Yes, I've learned my lesson and No, I would not go back on the party line or MySpace trying to find a date not knowing for sure if it's not them or not."

SCRAPBOOK
The Makings of M.V.P.

The Makings of M.V.P.

She was born a Pisces, on March 17th, St. Patrick's Day
Conceived by her mother, a Taurus, whose birthday is on the 18th of May
5 pounds, 15 ounces with the cutest slanted eyes
Wondering what this beautiful baby will grow to be, it was quite a surprise
So young and energetic at the age of 3
Always posing for the camera, as my dad took pictures
Of me
So photogenic and boyish, even way back then
The dominance of acting like being a boy began
At the age of 10, when she saw a TV special that showed women, dressed like a men
Very young and very curious to find out
What being like the opposite sex was all about?
A very good kid, but trouble began to follow
Beautiful and tomboyish on the outside, but her heart
Was very hollow
She hated wearing girl clothes and hung around
With nothing but boys
She started trading in her Barbie's for G.I. Joe toys
She then started stealing clothes from the boys she knew
After she put the clothes on she thought she was through
But she didn't have a clue
Sad to say, with the boy clothes on she went
Outside pretending to be a guy
Her friends tried to make fun of her, but she stood tall and didn't even cry
As she got older, she changed the way she looked and how she walked
During the transformations, her voice became very raspy when she talked

Her freshmen year, she met a group of girls that were just like her
She had no idea what different feelings they were about to stir
The females that she met introduced her to the Gay Life
Full of relief, even thought she knew her mother would say it's not right
So she kept it a secret from her family to see
'Cause if she would have told them, they wouldn't let her be
She denied it for as long as she could... until one day
Her mother went through her personal things and had something to say
Her mother found a shoebox that she hid under her bed
The things her mother found in it made her face turn red
She found love letters from a girl, cigarettes and a gay porno flick
The thought of her mother finding out that way really made her sick
She just stood there emotionless, wanting to melt
Disappointed and hurt, that's how she know her mother felt
Her mother wanted to hurt her, so she told her no more girls were allowed over again
Little did she know that the rebellion was about to begin
Just to be around her friends, she ran away from home
At first it was fun, but being away from her family made her feel like she was alone
She started doing odd jobs, just to get by
Then the thought of not being loved by her mother would then make her cry
She soon got tired from being in the streets; she was ready to go back to her mom's place
But she didn't want to deal with the disappointment on her mother's face
So she sucked in her pride and went back to mom's place

When she got there everyone was excited to see her, rather than full of disgrace
Ever since that day she and her mother have been very close
They actually work in the same building and her mom visits her at her post
"I can truly say my mother finally accepted me for who I was inside
'Cause the feelings that I have for women, I no longer have to hide
To people out there that's afraid to tell your family about your lifestyle, just be patient
And wait for the right time

Because you don't want them to find out the hard way
Like mine"

HEAD SHOT

A PAINTING OF ME

2009 HARDCANDY CALENDAR

HARDCANDY CALENDAR

GETTING TATTED UP

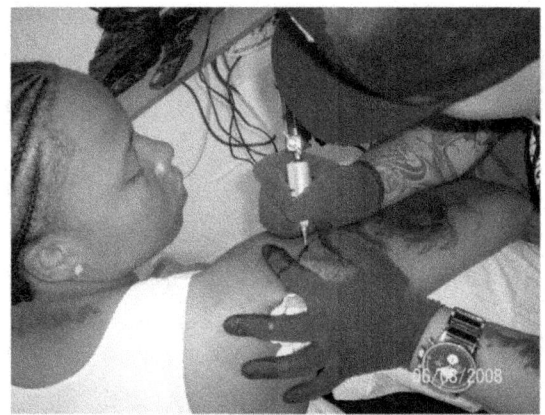

RIDING CLEAN

2008 GUN RANGE

SKY DIVING FOR THE FIRST TIME 5/2008

www.themakingsofmvp.com

www.ingramcontent.com/pod-product-compliance
Lightning Source LLC
LaVergne TN
LVHW021408080426
835508LV00020B/2506